RITA MORENO

A Tapestry of Triumph –
The Journey of an Icon

Alba Garrido Rico

Copyright @ 2024 By Alba Garrido Rico

All rights reserved. No part of this book may be reproduced, distributed, or transmitted in any form or by any means, including photocopying, recording, or other electronic or mechanical methods, without the prior written permission of the publisher, except in the case of brief quotations embodied in critical reviews and specific other noncommercial uses permitted by copyright law.

Content

INTRODUCTION

CHAPTER 1: EARLY LIFE
    Childhood in Puerto Rico
    Immigrating to the United States

CHAPTER 2: THE SPARK OF PERFORMANCE
    Discovering a Passion for Acting and Dance
    Early Stage Experiences

CHAPTER 3: HOLLYWOOD BREAKTHROUGH
    Casting in "West Side Story"
    Overcoming Stereotypes in Film

CHAPTER 4: A TRAILBLAZER FOR DIVERSITY
    Advocating for Representation
    Pioneering Roles in Television and Film

CHAPTER 5: BROADWAY AND BEYOND
    Achievements in Theater
    Collaborations with Renowned Artists

CHAPTER 6: AWARDS AND RECOGNITION
    Oscar, Emmy, and Tony Wins
    The Significance of EGOT

CHAPTER 7: PERSONAL LIFE AND CHALLENGES
    Balancing Fame and Family
    Overcoming Adversity
CHAPTER 8: LATER CAREER AND CONTINUED INFLUENCE
    Recent Projects and Activism
    Mentoring the Next Generation
CHAPTER 9: THE LEGACY OF RITA MORENO
    Impact on Arts and Culture
    Continuing Her Mission
CONCLUSION

INTRODUCTION

Every story has a hero's journey at its core, which is a tale of struggles, victories, and personal growth. Rita Moreno views that trip as more than just a personal triumph; it is a colorful tapestry made of strands of culture, enthusiasm, and tenacity. Rita's tale starts in a modest setting where the rich traditions of her family blended with the rhythms of Latin music, giving her a profound passion for the arts. However, this was only the setting for a life that would eventually smash stereotypes and rewrite the rules of what it meant to be a Latina in Hollywood.

Rita's family moved to the busy streets of New York City when she was a child; this would present both a hardship and an opportunity. She found her love of performing here, in the midst of the bustle of city life; this love would take her to dance classes, auditions, and the exciting world of theater. The neon lights of Broadway lighted her path, but there were many challenges along the way. During a period when actors of color in Hollywood were marginalized, Rita had to deal with a system that frequently tried to limit her ability to fit into preconceived notions. She battled these restrictions with such tenacity that she also started to change the stereotypes about Latina women in entertainment.

Rita's big break came from her legendary performance in the historic 1961 classic "West Side Story," as Anita. She gained widespread recognition at that point and became the first Latina actress to win an Academy Award. She also received critical accolades. Rita understood the responsibility that came with her increased notoriety, though and chose not to rest on her laurels. She realized that representing a community that had long been marginalized was more important to her achievement than merely achieving personal glory. She aimed to present complex, real people in every part she took on, shattering stereotypes about Latina women in the arts and opening doors for upcoming generations of performers.

Rita Moreno's journey is distinguished by her tenacity as well as her professional accomplishments. She struggled with the demands of stardom, the complexities of identity, and the demons of self-doubt behind the scenes. Rita had times of vulnerability that would have overwhelmed a weaker person since the bright lights of accomplishment frequently produced deep shadows. Her openness to discussing these things, including her issues with relationships and mental health, shows how real and complex her journey has been. Rita's transparency turns into a source of strength in a society where being vulnerable is frequently viewed as a weakness, showing that true courage is facing one's anxieties and accepting one's imperfections.

Rita has made significant contributions to art and social justice in addition to this, supporting Latino representation in the media and lending her voice to concerns of prejudice and inequality. Her dedication to activism is just as strong as her acting profession; she has not only advocated for her community but also put in countless hours to open doors for others. Rita now serves as a mentor to upcoming artists, encouraging them to share their own stories and accept their individuality. She has changed her own story via her activism, and she has made it possible for a great number of people to follow in her footsteps.

This biography explores the complex web of events that have molded Rita Moreno into an iconic figure. It goes far into her life. We shall travel through the landscapes of her successes and setbacks, from her early years in Puerto Rico to her ascent to prominence in Hollywood as a trailblazing actor. We'll look at the cultural relevance of her output and the lasting influence she has had on both society and the entertainment sector. Every chapter will shed light on the intricacies of her life, creating a thorough picture of a woman who has led an audacious and genuine existence.

Get ready to see a life that is a celebration of resiliency and creativity as we set off on our exploration. Rita Moreno is more than just a name; she is the embodiment of a community's spirit and a living example of the transformative power of art and the never-ending struggle for equality and representation. Her story is an inspiration to everyone who dares to dream big and defy the status quo. It serves as a reminder that every obstacle faced is a step toward writing a larger story and that every voice counts in the pursuit of justice and comprehension.

Learn about Rita Moreno's incredible life, which is full of purpose, passion, and the unyielding confidence that one person can truly change the world. Her life serves as a mirror for our setbacks and victories, serving as a reminder that the path of an artist is not only an individual one but also a communal one that unites the aspirations of all those who aspire to be acknowledged and acknowledged. Let's honor the legacy of a woman who has not only amused us but also encouraged us to embrace our identities and speak up for our truths as we turn the pages of her incredible journey.

CHAPTER 1: EARLY LIFE

Childhood in Puerto Rico

The early years Rita Moreno spent in Puerto Rico were woven together by a rich tapestry of family, culture, and life lessons that would later influence her identity and artistic career. Born on December 11, 1931, as Rosa Dolores Alverío in Humacao, a seaside town renowned for its colorful customs and rich surroundings, Rita's early years were filled with the warmth of her family and the rhythms of Caribbean life. She was raised in a poor home by her parents, Francisco and Rosa Alverío, who taught her the importance of perseverance, hard work, and creativity.

The sounds and colors of Puerto Rican culture permeated the home. Her early years were greatly influenced by music; the catchy tunes of salsa, plena, and boleros served as a constant background during this time. Rita's mother, who also wanted to be a dancer, saw her daughter's potential at a young age and urged her to pursue a career in performing. Rita's deep love of the arts was cultivated in this caring atmosphere, which gave her the freedom to express herself via dance and music—two mediums that were essential to her cultural identity.

Rita grew up in a vibrant neighborhood that had get-togethers and festivals to honor its culture. She was deeply impacted by the colorful fiestas, which were full of traditional cuisine, music, and dancing and gave her a strong sense of pride in her heritage. These festivities were more than just events; they served as potent declarations of identity and community. Rita, who was fascinated by the power of performance to unite people and communicate tales, used to dream of a life on stage while watching her family perform traditional dances at these gatherings.

But there were difficulties in Puerto Rican life as well. When Rita was just five years old, her parents had to make the difficult decision to move to New York City in search of better possibilities due to financial troubles in the family. This move put her out of the comfortable embrace of her island home and into the busy, sometimes overwhelming environment of a large metropolis, marking a turning point in her life. Although there were many unknowns associated with the transfer, there was also hope for new opportunities that would eventually lead to her artistic career.

Rita was first struck by the sharp contrast between New York and her birthplace upon her arrival. The city's fast speed and tall skyscrapers were thrilling and terrifying at the same time. Rita had to adjust to a new language and culture as her family moved into a small apartment in the East Harlem district. Although she grew up speaking Spanish at home, she soon recognized that in order to function in her new school setting, she needed to learn English. Although she was intimidated by the language barrier, it gave her a new way to express her will and creativity.

The school was a place of learning and challenges. Rita had a hard time getting started in a setting where most people spoke English, but she quickly realized that her passion for performing could bring people together. She would take part in school productions and neighborhood talent shows, frequently captivating her peers with her contagious enthusiasm and innate skill. These early encounters greatly influenced her confidence and her love of the performing arts.

Rita's familial relationships had a big impact on her during her early years. Her ambitious attitude was sparked by her father's strong work ethic and her mother's steadfast support. Rita would frequently talk about the sacrifices her parents made for their family, working nonstop to make sure their kids had the best chances. This commitment had a profound effect on her and inspired her to achieve in a field that was famously challenging for women, particularly women of color.

Rita had happy and enlightening childhood experiences in addition to the struggles. Captivated by the opulent lifestyles of Hollywood celebrities, she would frequently withdraw herself into the world of cinema. Her ambition to pursue acting was further stoked by the silver screen, which served as a source of inspiration and ignited her imagination. Her early dreams included acting and rewriting the history of Latina actresses, with the goal of one day being able to represent her culture on a national platform.

Rita's identification as a Latina artist was greatly influenced by her experiences growing up in Puerto Rico and then living in New York. Her rich cultural background and the harsh realities of being an immigrant were juxtaposed to give her a distinct perspective that she would use throughout her career. Her artistic expression is rooted in a blend of influences, including her island upbringing, her family's challenges, and the dynamic arts environment of New York. This blend enables her to gracefully and resiliently manage the complexity of her identity.

Immigrating to the United States

At the infant age of five, Rita Moreno's immigration to the United States caused a profound upheaval in her life and permanently changed the course of her future. Moving would not only be a simple change of scenery; it would be a profound shift that would introduce her to a new language and culture and rekindle her passionate will to succeed in the face of adversity.

Rita's parents made the tough choice to move to New York City in 1936 as financial difficulties and a lack of opportunity in Puerto Rico threatened to spoil their kids. The family left behind the beautiful scenery and dynamic culture of their native country and set out on an uncertain trip. This meant leaving behind the warm music that filled family gatherings, the familiar embrace of her relatives, and the reassuring regularity of island life for young Rita.

Rita was thrown into an exciting and daunting buzzing metropolis when she arrived in New York. The serene beauty of Humacao was dramatically contrasted with the vibrant city. The beautiful slopes of Puerto Rico gave way to towering skyscrapers, and the din of metropolitan life produced a backdrop that was both fascinating and intimidating. Rita had a difficult time adjusting to the realities of an English-speaking educational system due to the language barrier. She struggled to connect and interact with her friends, who were engrossed in a world she was starting to grasp, and she frequently felt alone.

Rita found solace in the customs of her Puerto Rican background during those early years. Her family's joyful, dance-filled get-togethers turned into revered customs that supported her through the rough seas of transition. She was able to express herself in a language that went beyond words during this time of change, thanks to her mother's encouragement to dance and perform. Dancing turned to become a haven, a means for her to stay connected to her heritage and express her feelings in a strange and demanding setting.

Rita's parents put in a lot of overtime to support their family when they moved into a small apartment in East Harlem. Her mother, who had her own goals in the arts, remained a constant source of support, even while her father worked many jobs. Young Rita was aware of their sacrifices and learned from their adversity and resiliency that hard work and determination were necessary for success. She was motivated to follow her own goals despite obstacles by their unwavering perseverance.

The school turned into a battlefield. Rita struggled to maintain her cultural identity while adjusting to the constraints of fitting in. She frequently felt like an outcast because of the sharp contrast between her Puerto Rican background and her largely Anglo-American surroundings. She, nevertheless, resisted allowing these difficulties to break her spirit. Rita, on the other hand, found comfort in the performing arts and used her developing skills to make a name for herself. She found solace in talent shows and school plays, which gave her an opportunity to shine and briefly break free from the bonds of her fears.

Notwithstanding the challenges, Rita's worldview was significantly shaped by New York City's lively diversity. She was exposed to a variety of languages, customs, and artistic expressions thanks to the city's multiculturalism. She started to see the value of narrative as a connecting tool and the beauty of diversity. Her horizons were expanded by this exposure, which fueled her ambition to excel personally and to represent her culture more widely.

Rita became very aware of the misconceptions that frequently beset Latina actresses as she managed the difficulties of immigrant life. She felt a sense of responsibility after coming to this conclusion because she realized that she was part of a bigger story that needed to be questioned and revised, not just a single person following her ambitions. She tried to break free from the constraints imposed on her by a culture that frequently limited Latina women to one-dimensional roles with every performance. Rita had aspirations not only for herself but also for the next wave of artists who would come after her.

Rita began her career as an entertainment professional in the late 1940s and early 1950s. She made the unshakeable decision to pursue acting and dancing despite her youth. She seized every chance that presented her, frequently going on auditions for parts that represented the nuanced fabric of her identity. Though it wasn't easy, this goal helped her land tiny roles in TV shows and movies. Rita kept running into the same prejudices that she was trying to break because the industry at the time was so full of typecasting. Every turndown and prejudice fed her flames, intensifying her desire to rewrite the rules on what it meant to be a Latina in Hollywood.

Rita Moreno's story, told via her experiences as an immigrant in America, is a tribute to tenacity, flexibility, and the unwavering pursuit of aspirations. Her early hardships in New York created a resilient attitude that would eventually help her achieve career highs never seen before. Rita became a cultural icon as well as an artist, personifying the intricacies of identity and the transforming potential of narrative. Her advocacy was shaped by her experience as an immigrant, which gave her the confidence to question the existing quo and encourage others to embrace their ancestry proudly.

CHAPTER 2: THE SPARK OF PERFORMANCE

Discovering a Passion for Acting and Dance

Rita Moreno's path into the performing and dance arts was more than just a search for creative expression; it was a profoundly personal epiphany that entwined her goals, aspirations, and the colorful energy of her environment. She was exposed to music and dancing at a young age because her family respected the arts. But her interest really took off in the busy streets and vibrant neighborhoods of New York City.

Rita found that the hectic pace of city life after the family moved from Puerto Rico was both a challenge and an inspiration. Her early school experiences, which were difficult due to linguistic and cultural differences, left her looking for a sense of community and belonging. It was in this period that she first became aware of the transformative potential of theater. Rita was a regular participant in school talent events when she first discovered that dancing and acting might serve as creative and expressive outlets.

She had never felt this sensation of independence until she went onto the improvised stages of school auditoriums. She was excited about singing in front of an audience because it gave her a sense of community, an opportunity to shine, and a chance to share experiences that went beyond her regular existence. She was able to overcome her fears as a young immigrant girl with each dance and every word spoken on stage. She found refuge on stage, transforming her emotions into art, and her inherent talent and energy captivated both her professors and peers.

Rita's love for dancing grew as she pursued professional instruction. She took classes in ballet, jazz, and traditional dances from Puerto Rico, among other forms, which expanded her creative horizons. Her background shaped her as a performer by providing her with a foundation in the rhythms and motions that resonated with her identity. Rita saw dance as more than simply a discipline; it was a means of honoring the culture she brought with her and an essential link to her heritage.

Rita also became acquainted with the world of acting through dancing. She had to take on character roles in many of her early performances, using her creativity and storytelling abilities. Her ability to explore complicated emotions and themes was made possible by the duality of dance and acting. She became aware as she spun and jumped that every action had a meaning, often expressing emotions that words alone were unable to capture. This understanding was crucial since it confirmed her desire to become a professional performer.

Rita's growing passion for the theater was noted. Her mother urged her to try out for professional chances after realizing her talent. Rita got her mother's persistent backing as she started navigating the cutthroat world of show business. She went to local theaters to try out for parts, and over time, she established herself in New York's thriving artistic scene. Every audition presented a fresh chance for her to shine in the limelight and display her special talents.

Rita persevered in pursuing her goals in spite of a lot of rejections, which frequently felt demoralizing. She quickly discovered that there were many difficulties in the entertainment business, especially for Latina actresses. But rather than letting these setbacks stop her, she utilized them as inspiration to get better at what she did. Her will to achieve turned into a motivating factor that forced her to put in more effort and improve her abilities.

Rita had started laying the groundwork for her career by the time she reached her teenage years. She was cast in a number of theater shows, where she received exposure and invaluable experience. Talent scouts were drawn to her shows because of their dynamic energy, which enthralled audiences. Opportunity started to present itself to her as a result of her undeniable talent and contagious personality.

The pivotal moment occurred when Rita received an offer for her first movie role, a little part in the 1950 picture "So Young, So Bad." Despite playing a small part, the job signaled her official debut in the film industry—a desire she had long nurtured. This first encounter stoked a passion in her and confirmed her decision to make acting and dancing her career. It was thrilling to be on set, collaborate with seasoned performers, and be a part of a bigger artistic endeavor.

Rita continued to hone her dancing abilities, showing her talent in front of audiences in smaller, more personal settings at clubs and events throughout town. Her unique style, which distinguished her in a field dominated by conventional conventions, was the blending of dance and acting. She discovered how to incorporate her dance training into her acting, giving her acting the same enthusiasm and liveliness she brought to the stage.

Rita's career would inevitably come to a crossroads as her notoriety expanded. She struggled to live up to Hollywood's limited standards for Latina actresses. But rather than caving into prejudice, she embraced her identity and turned it into a strength. She realized that by bringing honesty and nuance to her parts, her distinct background opened the door for more nuanced representations of Latina women in movies.

Rita's pursuit of her passion for dancing and acting was not just about her happiness; it was also about representation and changing the perception of Latina actors in Hollywood. She not only followed her ambitions with each part she took on, but she also made room for those who, like her, were sometimes overlooked in the entertainment world.

Rita Moreno showed that passion, tenacity, and inventiveness could dismantle obstacles and light the way for coming generations by turning her childhood goals into a lifetime purpose via her dedication to her profession. Her journey from New York's dance halls to the big screen served as a testament to the strength of accepting one's identity and pursuing one's passion; this story would resound throughout her incredible career.

Early Stage Experiences

Rita Moreno's early experiences were pivotal since they not only molded her artistic personality but also gave her the fortitude required to handle the challenges of an entertainment industry career. The young actress was driven to make her mark in the exciting world of theater after relocating to New York City, where opportunities abound but obstacles are formidable.

Rita's first steps into the performing arts were accompanied by apprehension and exhilaration. She got involved in neighborhood theater plays and learned the value of working with other creatives who were as passionate about presenting stories as she was. She learned the value of cooperation and the potential for magic when imaginative minds came together from these experiences. She took part in a number of community plays, developing her craft and self-assurance. Every show offered her an opportunity to try new things, delve into new personas, and interact with viewers; this sense of accomplishment fed her drive.

Her first major theatrical experience was with the esteemed company "New York Theatre Workshop." Rita discovered herself encircled by a wide range of abilities in this place, each person contributing their distinct viewpoints and approaches to the stage. She was motivated to exceed her limits as an actress and dancer by the collaborative environment. She eagerly jumped into a variety of parts, from dramatic to humorous, and learned something new about herself and her profession from each one. Her ability to think quickly, adjust to the audience's enthusiasm, and accept the unpredictability of live performances were all necessary due to the intense nature of live theater.

Rita faced the harsh reality of a business that frequently ignored musicians of color in addition to the thrill of performing on stage. She was confronted with a plethora of preconceptions early in her career that threatened to define her. Latina women were usually restricted to supporting or caricature roles, which were frequently shallow and uncomplicated. Her ambition to question the existing quo and look for parts that would allow her to play complex characters was fueled by this fact. She started to realize at this point how crucial it is for artists to represent many voices and how storytelling affects how others view a culture.

Rita's dedication to her profession was noted. She started to become more well-known after being cast in several noteworthy projects. Her performance in the Broadway production of "Skydrift," a musical that highlighted her extraordinary aptitude for both acting and dancing, was one noteworthy event. Her ability to showcase her diversity and adaptability during the production was a turning point in her career. She was recognized as a rising star in the theater industry by critics who appreciated her performance. She started to thrive in this supportive and encouraging atmosphere, gaining self-assurance and securing her position in the performing arts world.

Rita started pursuing her interests in theater and joined the "Young People's Theatre," where she assisted with production administration in addition to acting. Through this experience, she gained vital knowledge about the inner workings of theater, including production design, stage management, and the teamwork needed to make a performance happen. Her grasp of the industry was expanded by her diverse education, which made it possible for her to recognize the wide range of roles that go into making theater.

Rita was first introduced to the power of storytelling through her early-stage experiences. She has direct experience with the power of narratives to move audiences, arouse feelings, and start discussions. This insight sparked a deep desire to represent characters who captured the complexity of the human condition, particularly those that paralleled her own experiences as a Latina woman. She started looking for parts that would let her tell important stories in the hopes that her performances would uplift people and subvert social standards.

Rita encountered the unavoidable obstacles that come with being an artist as she worked to hone her skills. There were times when I doubted myself, especially in light of the demands and constraints of the industry. She didn't waver in her determination to forge a route that truly spoke to her, though. Her early experiences, which were both rewarding and difficult, served as the cornerstone for her future professional endeavors. They gave her a feeling of direction and the conviction that her work could effect change.

Her first major film part in "So Young, So Bad," where she brought the same passion and commitment she had developed on stage, was the pinnacle of her early stage experiences. She had to modify her performances to fit the subtle needs of the camera, which made the move from theater to film difficult. Nevertheless, the abilities she had honed in the theater prepared her for this new platform, enabling her to transform her fascinating stage persona into captivating cinematic roles.

Rita Moreno's formative years played a crucial role in defining both her artistic and personal identities. They instilled in her the virtues of tenacity, the significance of representation, and the transforming potential of narrative. Every part she performed in and every platform she walked on helped her on her path to being a trailblazer in the film industry. These formative experiences gave her a profound respect for the arts and a strong desire to utilize her platform to uplift others, which ultimately helped her pursue a career that would change the landscape of what was possible for Latina actresses in the entertainment business.

CHAPTER 3: HOLLYWOOD BREAKTHROUGH

Casting in "West Side Story"

Rita Moreno's "West Side Story" casting marked a turning point in her career as well as in the larger scheme of American representation in film. The stage was set for a musical adaptation of the movie that would ultimately change the theater and cinema industries as the picture was ready for production in the late 1950s. That being said, the road to landing her legendary role as Anita was far from easy.

Rita had established herself as a successful actress through theater and a number of cinema roles by that point. Her reputation was also expanding. Nevertheless, her possibilities were frequently restricted by Hollywood's limiting perceptions of Latina actresses. Stereotypes were pervasive in the industry, and there were very few jobs available for women of color. Upon her casting call for "West Side Story," Rita realized that her performance might potentially transform not just her own life but also the way Latinas are portrayed in movies.

A wide range of talented people applied to be considered for the role of the "West Side Story" characters, and all of them were influenced by Shakespeare's "Romeo and Juliet." Rita had a tough audition, but the producers and director Robert Wise were drawn to her natural charisma, strong voice, and dynamic dancing abilities. Rita gave Anita a genuineness that captured the complexity of being a Puerto Rican immigrant in America. Anita was a powerful and sensitive heroine.

The casting crew realized how crucial it was to find an actress who could accurately portray the character's cultural background in addition to being a gifted actor. Rita was a perfect choice because of her expertise in ballet and theater, but what really won them over was her intense portrayal of Anita. She brought an indisputably alive vitality to the role throughout her audition, highlighting the journey's innate power and sensitivity.

Rita knew just how much was at stake, even in the midst of the casting frenzy. The goal of the ground-breaking film "West Side Story" was to portray a moving tale of racial tensions and cultural conflicts in America. The movie's potential to connect with viewers would determine its success, and Rita was aware that her performance would be closely scrutinized. She was taking on a role more than just acting; she was taking on a position of authority and representing her community in a way never seen in a production of this magnitude.

Rita was engulfed in the team spirit of the actors and staff as soon as rehearsals got underway. She had never seen anything like the Jerome Robbins-created choreography before. It tested her limits as a performer and required a degree of skill and expressiveness that she had never experienced before. Each dance routine was painstakingly created to portray the characters' colorful cultures by fusing street dancing enthusiasm with classical ballet. Rita accepted the challenge and used her personal experiences as a Latina woman to inform her portrayal, making Anita a highly relatable character for the audience.

The song "America," which features Rita's character Anita and her fellow cast members navigating issues of identity, longing, and the immigrant experience, was a turning point in the movie. The words and choreography emphasized the differences between Puerto Rican living and the imagined glitz of America. Rita's rendition of this song was more than simply a demonstration of her technical prowess; it was a sincere portrayal of the difficulties associated with belonging and ambition. Her ability to portray a range of feelings, from happiness to annoyance, struck a deep chord with both reviewers and viewers.

Rita Moreno played Anita in the movie, which debuted in 1961 and went on to become famous. She became the first Latina to win an Oscar when she took home the Best Supporting Actress trophy. This significant acknowledgment opened possibilities for upcoming generations of Latina actors and marked a change in Hollywood's casting and representation practices. Rita's accomplishment was more than just a one-person triumph; it was a group effort for a community that the entertainment business had marginalized for a long time.

However, the trip had its successes. Rita understood that this prominence presented a chance to push for more accurate and diverse representations of Latina women. She took advantage of her position to confront the persistent Hollywood prejudices. She put great effort into guaranteeing that parts of the future will accurately represent the depth and diversity of the Latino experience.

Her role in "West Side Story" changed the course of her career and the industry as a whole. It illustrated the value of representation and the capacity of narrative to cross-cultural barriers. Rita's transformation into Anita became a ray of hope, encouraging a generation of young artists to follow their passions and serving as a reminder that they, too, could make a name for themselves in a society that frequently tried to exclude them.

Overcoming Stereotypes in Film

Rita Moreno's career in Hollywood is not only a tale of accomplishments on a personal level; it is also a story of resistance to and victory against deeply ingrained preconceptions that have historically suppressed Latina actors. Rita's career path became a potent counter-narrative, changing what it meant to be a Latina in American cinema at a period when the film business restricted women of color to simple roles.

The entertainment industry was rife with stereotypes of Latina women when Rita arrived in the late 1940s and early 1950s. Characters were frequently shown as overly sexualized, submissive, or one-dimensional, devoid of complexity or free will. Rita's rich cultural heritage was not honored, nor did these representations capture the complex reality of the Latino experience. As a gifted young actress, she had to negotiate a difficult environment where there were few options and mostly stereotypical roles.

Knowing the terrain, Rita first took on parts that matched expectations in the industry. She soon saw, though, that doing so would not further her artistic goals or benefit her community. She understood that in every job, it was necessary to dispel the stereotypes that limited Latina actors. Rita made a brave and dangerous decision, but her persistent will to change her story propelled her.

Her casting in "West Side Story" marked a turning moment in her fight against stereotypes. Anita was a figure rooted in her cultural background, but she also reflected strength and depth, qualities that were sometimes missing from representations of Latina women. Rita gave Anita dimension by creating a performance that was nuanced and real. Her two-dimensional portrayals that had previously

39

dominated the screen were a long cry from the part that allowed her to showcase the color and vitality of Latina identity.

Rita understood that she would have to live up to some expectations, even as she welcomed the chance to portray Anita. She had to strike a careful balance between defending her identity and resisting the constrictive notions Hollywood imposed. This conflict brought to light a larger problem facing the industry: there has to be more varied voices represented behind the scenes as well as in front of the camera. Rita's achievement was a result of a greater struggle for visibility and authenticity that called for group effort rather than just her own.

After her breakthrough performance in "West Side Story," Rita encountered both praise and criticism. Her performance earned her an Academy Award, which cemented her reputation as a trailblazer but also put her under scrutiny. The expectation of representing not only herself but the entire Latino community accompanied her increased exposure. Rita was aware of the duty that came with it, and she made use of it to push for more diverse and significant depictions of Latina women in movies. She started looking for roles that went against popular assumptions and pushed for storylines that showed the whole range of Latino experiences, including happiness, suffering, struggle, and victory.

Rita broke down barriers all over again throughout the 1970s and 1980s, not letting herself be defined by convention. She accepted a wide range of roles in movies and television, which gave her the chance to play nuanced characters. Rita's acting ability was showcased through her work on the critically acclaimed television program "The Electric Company" and her numerous guest appearances in other programs. She also engaged in socially conscious projects, addressing topics like immigration, identity, and cultural pride with her platform.

Rita's openness to voice her disapproval of the faults in the sector served as even more evidence of her resolve.

She became an outspoken supporter of increased representation, emphasizing time and time again the necessity for real stories that truly captured the realities of Latinos in America. Rita committed to mentoring young artists who aspired to be like her because she believed that her voice could affect change. She inspired the next generation to embrace their ancestry, challenge preconceptions, and share their tales through seminars, presentations, and one-on-one mentoring.

Rita's advocacy went beyond the performing industry; she started working with writers and filmmakers to create productions that highlighted Latina viewpoints. She realized that diverse storytelling and casting were necessary for real transformation. She wanted to provide complexity, comedy, and humanity—aspects that had been glaringly absent in earlier portrayals—space in the stories centered around Latina characters by actively participating in their development.

The struggle against stereotypes in Hollywood persisted despite the advancements. Rita had periods of disappointment and annoyance when she came across initiatives that continued antiquated clichés. Her tenacity, nevertheless, never faltered. She persisted in pressuring filmmakers, producers, and authors to adopt a broader perspective on Latina women, advocating for authenticity in storytelling and casting.

Rita's perseverance paid off, leaving a legacy that motivated viewers and artists alike. Her dedication to shattering stereotypes made it possible for upcoming generations of Latina actresses to take pride in their presence in Hollywood. The stereotypes about Latina women started to change as more varied voices entered the field. The popularity of television programs and movies with nuanced, multifaceted Latina characters indicated that the depth of Latino lives and narratives was becoming increasingly acknowledged.

CHAPTER 4: A TRAILBLAZER FOR DIVERSITY

Advocating for Representation

Rita Moreno's career is evidence of her tremendous talent, as well as her steadfast dedication to promoting diversity in the entertainment industry. Being a trailblazer in Hollywood, she has fought relentlessly against the prejudices and structural obstacles that have historically silenced the voices of Latina actresses and the larger Latino community.

Rita realized early on in the 1960s and later on that her prominence might have a significant effect on how Latina women were viewed in the media. Even though she was successful, she understood that her path was connected to the hardships of those in her community who did not have the same possibilities. She believed it was her natural duty to not only achieve personal success but also to open doors for upcoming performers. Her activism was driven by this awareness, which compelled her to support more accurate representations of Latinos in media.

Rita's activism really got going in the late 1960s, when social justice and civil rights movements gained national attention. Rita recognized a chance to connect her career path with a larger cultural movement as underrepresented groups started to demand a voice in society. She started advocating against the absence of parts for Latina actors and actresses, calling into question Hollywood's pervasive practice of damaging stereotypes and typecasting.

Rita's involvement in forums and public talks addressing representational concerns was one of her most important platforms. She was a strong critic of the television and film industries, frequently pointing out that there weren't enough Latina women in parts that represented the complexity and richness of their lives. Rita made it quite evident that the way Latinos were portrayed in the media needed to change, going beyond cliches that fell short of truly capturing the diversity of their cultures.

In an attempt to bring about change, Rita worked with a number of groups that supported diversity in the arts. She participated in programs aimed at empowering young Latina artists and inspiring them to overcome obstacles in order to achieve their goals. Rita offered her experiences and wisdom through seminars, community outreach, and mentorship programs, assisting in the development of a new generation of artists who would question the existing quo.

Rita's advocacy also affected the roles she chose to play; she started to be pickier about the people she chose to play. She championed scripts that addressed themes of cultural heritage, resilience, and empowerment, actively seeking out projects that highlighted the complex and multidimensional character of Latina identities. She improved her career and gave others a platform to tell their stories by accepting these kinds of storytelling.

A turning point in her campaign was while "West Side Story" was being produced. Even though Rita received a great deal of attention for her portrayal of Anita, she was acutely conscious of the need for more inclusive storytelling that featured Latino voices. She made use of her status to advocate for authentic representation following the film's release, emphasizing the value of well-rounded, multifaceted characters who accurately reflected their real-life experiences. Rita stated unequivocally that the popularity of "West Side Story" ought to serve as a spur for improvements in the representation of Latina characters rather than a singular occurrence.

In the decades that followed, Rita's dedication to activism grew even stronger. She rose to prominence in conversations about diversity in Hollywood, participating in panels and interviews where she pushed the business to own up to its part in influencing public opinion. She persistently pushed studios and production companies to adopt a more inclusive casting and storytelling strategy, and she promoted hiring methods that represented the diversity of America.

Rita used her platform to promote change within the industry in addition to giving speeches in public. She participated in efforts to increase representation in front of and behind the camera by serving on a number of boards and committees that addressed diversity in the arts. Rita realized that real change would need more visibility as well as the participation of other viewpoints in the procedures that determine how the entertainment industry is shaped.

Rita's own producing activities served to amplify her cause further. Her goal was to produce projects that highlighted Latino talent and stories, realizing that true representation could only come about when artists were given the chance to share their tales. Rita wanted to make sure that the tales being conveyed were not just representative but also poignant and meaningful, so she supported scripts written by Latino writers and involved Latino filmmakers.

Rita remained dedicated to intersectionality in her advocacy throughout her journey. She understood that the struggle for representation touched on issues of gender, sexual orientation, and socioeconomic class in addition to ethnicity. Rita took an inclusive stance when it came to activism, supporting the inclusion of all underrepresented voices in the media. She was aware that in order to achieve true equity in Hollywood, numerous levels of prejudice and discrimination would need to be addressed, and she devoted her life to raising awareness of these problems.

Rita Moreno's voice on inclusivity and representation has continued to be an essential component of the discourse that has been gaining traction in Hollywood in recent years. She keeps calling for reform and speaking out against injustices, reminding the media that it must represent the variety of its viewership. Her confidence in the ability of storytelling to change people's lives and communities is even more passionate than her unrelenting commitment to representation.

Rita left a lasting legacy as a supporter of representation in movies. Her experience is a testament to the fortitude of innumerable artists who have struggled against societal restrictions and preconceptions that limit their potential. Rita has paved the way for a new wave of Latina actresses and artists by defying the expectations of her day and speaking out for change. Her body of work is a constant reminder of the importance of representation, not only for the audiences who yearn to see themselves represented on television but also for the artists who want to share their experiences.

Pioneering Roles in Television and Film

Beyond just receiving critical praise, Rita Moreno's groundbreaking performances in movies and television changed the entertainment industry, particularly for women of color. Rita was a trailblazer who broke through the rigid and destructive preconceptions Hollywood had placed on Latino performers, defying the limitations of her day. Rita was adamant about showcasing the depth and breadth of her talent, refusing to be constrained by stereotypes in a field where typecasting predominated. Her success in movies and television wasn't only a personal triumph; it also marked a turning point in media culture history and permanently altered how Latinas are portrayed on screen.

Rita had to deal painfully in the early years of her career with the fact that Hollywood frequently viewed her ethnicity as a liability rather than an advantage. The movie business regularly cast Latino actors in limited parts during the 1950s and 1960s, perpetuating negative stereotypes by casting them as either extremely exoticized, obedient, or evil. Rita realized she needed to fight against these constrictive portrayals if she wanted to have a lasting influence because these roles did not adequately represent the diversity of Latino cultures or the depth of the human experience. Not only did she need to demonstrate her versatility as an actor, but she also needed to stand up for parts that offered her depth and dignity. Her ambition and tenacity inspired her to embark on endeavors that would challenge her abilities and break down barriers for those who came after her.

Rita's performance as Anita in the 1961 motion picture "West Side Story" was one of her first big-screen highlights. This was more than just a career-defining role—it transformed the perception of Latina women in Hollywood. Rita was brilliant, lively, and fiercely independent in her portrayal of Anita. For the first time, a Latina character's strength, passion, and complexity were what distinguished her rather than her subservience or passive exoticism. With her sharp mind, her steadfast devotion, and her ability to balance tragedy and love, Anita became a legendary figure in film history. As the first Latina to win the Academy Award for Best Supporting Actress, Rita made history with her performance. More importantly, though, it proved that audiences were eager for characters with depth and relatability, and it opened possibilities for all Latino performers as well as for her.

Rita persisted in pushing the limits of the roles that were available to her after "West Side Story." Following her Oscar victory, she discovered that she was declining multiple parts that reflected the same prejudice she had fought so hard to break. Refusing to fit into a mold, she patiently awaited roles that would allow her to develop her artistic vision, even if it meant going through periods of artistic dry spells. Rita distinguished herself from many of her peers by having the guts to say "no" when it was most needed, and it also showed how dedicated she was to improving the way Latinos are portrayed in the media.

Her dedication to dispelling misconceptions carried over to television. Rita joined the cast of the children's educational television series "The Electric Company" in the 1970s, and she quickly rose to the top of the cast. She wasn't portraying a Latina character here; rather, she was a gifted performer who could enthrall audiences with her charm and comedy. Her presence transcended her nationality. Her role in "The Electric Company" introduced her to an entirely new audience, and both parents and children enjoyed her lively yet commanding manner. Her success in the show led to an Emmy Award, which solidified her reputation as a versatile actor who can shine in any setting.

Rita kept pushing boundaries in her work on television. Her ability to inhabit characters with depth, intelligence, and grit was demonstrated in her recurring part in the crime drama "The Rockford Files" in the late 1970s. She then went on to play a comic character in the sitcom "9 to 5," which was based on the well-known movie and addressed contemporary office interactions and feminist themes. Each television part cemented her status as a cultural icon she played, demonstrating her ability to blend comedy and serious acting deftly.

As Sister Peter Marie Reimondo in HBO's trailblazing prison drama "Oz," which dealt with tough subjects like violence, morality, and redemption, Rita took on a fresh task in the 1990s. Rita was a serene, multifaceted nun who gave convict counseling while frequently battling her inner demons in a program renowned for its grim realism. She had clearly continued to grow as an actress because this character was very different from anything she had ever done. Rita was demonstrating that genius knows no age and that she could reinvent herself in any century at a time when many actors find themselves marginalized. "Oz" demonstrated her capacity to reach deep emotional depths, adding even more dimension to her already remarkable career.

Rita was breaking new ground even in her older years. She played Lydia Riera, the opinionated and lively grandma, in the comedy "One Day at a Time," which is centered around a Cuban-American family. Rita's character added heart and humor to the screen, and the show was praised for its accurate portrayal of Latino culture. With Rita leading numerous emotionally charged sequences, the show addressed modern social concerns, including immigration, mental health, and identity. Her performance as Lydia was a virtuoso in fusing humor with feeling, winning her accolades from both reviewers and viewers and demonstrating once more that her career in television was far from done.

Rita Moreno changed the way that the television and cinema industries perceived race, culture, and representation in a profound way. Her groundbreaking performances in these fields went beyond simply breaking into a sector that was hostile to diversity. Rita demonstrated grace, talent, and unwavering fearlessness in every character she played, thereby expanding the boundaries of what performers of color could do. She cleared the path, making room for a new generation of performers to follow in her footsteps rather than merely paving it. In addition to demonstrating her extraordinary talent, her contributions to the arts also reflect her relentless quest for equality and representation in a society in dire need of both.

CHAPTER 5: BROADWAY AND BEYOND

Achievements in Theater

Rita Moreno's theatrical accomplishments serve as a cornerstone of her storied career, demonstrating her extraordinary adaptability and dedication to the performing arts. Rita's contributions to theater, from her early years in New York City to her well-received performances on stages all around the world, have not only emphasized her great skill but also functioned as a potent tool for advocacy and cultural representation.

Rita's career in theater started soon after her family relocated to New York City in the late 1930s. She was enthralled with the city's thriving cultural environment, and it was here that she developed her skills. Rita swiftly established herself in the musical theater industry thanks to her remarkable talent and strong work ethic. Her compelling charisma and natural ability to connect with audiences marked her early performances, which made her a rising star in a crowded field.

Rita's Broadway portrayal of one of the leads in "The King and I" was one of her first significant theatrical triumphs. She demonstrated her ability to portray nuanced emotions through movement and music in her portrayal of Tuptim, a role that required both vocal skill and emotional depth. Her status as a formidable performer was cemented by the experience, which also gave her a forum to discuss the underrepresentation of Latina artists in mainstream theater.

Rita kept pushing the envelope in her theatrical pursuits during the 1950s and 60s. She played leading parts in shows that demonstrated her versatility as an actor, including serious parts and upbeat musical numbers. She performed the classic character of Anita in the original Broadway production of "West Side Story," which is one of her most notable accomplishments. This was a crucial role since it gave her the chance to play a powerful, complex character who defied the common assumptions about Latina women in theater.

Rita's performance in "West Side Story" was revolutionary in terms of both artistic quality and societal impact. She vividly portrayed the intricacies of a young Puerto Rican lady balancing identity, love, and devotion in a contentious racial setting in her role as Anita. Her moving performances of hits like "America" came to represent the show; she combined a dynamic dance routine with her amazing vocals to enthrall viewers. She received a great deal of praise for the part, which solidified her place as a prominent player in American theater.

Rita's career in theater went much beyond "West Side Story," with several genre-spanning shows to her credit. In roles like "The Electric Company," where she mentored new performers in addition to acting, she demonstrated her flexibility. The program showcased Rita's dedication to using her platform to inform and inspire upcoming generations by fusing entertainment with educational information. Her performance in the show demonstrated to young audiences that people from different backgrounds could succeed in the arts, underscoring the significance of representation.

Rita actively worked to provide opportunities for other Latino performers; therefore, her influence on theater extended beyond her performances. She started speaking out against discrimination in casting and pushed theaters to consider a wider variety of voices and viewpoints. Her dedication to serving as a mentor and support system for young performers from marginalized areas was a reflection of her conviction that theater ought to be an inclusive platform.

Rita expanded her influence in the theatrical industry by dabbling in producing and directing in addition to her on-stage activities. She chose to work on projects that gave her the chance to highlight varied tales and question the conventional narratives presented in popular theater. As a result of her leadership, other artists were given the chance to share their stories, ensuring that the diverse range of Latino culture was well-represented in the performing arts.

Rita's reputation as a renowned performer has been cemented by the many honors she has garnered for her services to theater over her career. Her performance in "The Ritz" earned her the Tony Award for Best Featured Actress in a Musical, which highlighted her skill and commitment to the field. Rita has become a beloved character in the theater world thanks to her captivating stage presence and support of diversity.

Rita was dedicated to investigating new theater forms even as she developed as an artist. She used her artistic expression to interact with current concerns and stimulate conversation while taking part in innovative productions that tackled societal challenges. Her performances resonated with viewers on a personal level because they frequently reflected her own experiences as a Latina woman in America.

Rita's accomplishments in theater go beyond her solo shows; they are part of a larger trend in the arts toward diversity and inclusivity. Numerous artists have been motivated by her story to follow their passions and support representation, and this influence is still felt in the theater industry today. Rita has not only made a name for herself but also created opportunities for upcoming performers by dismantling obstacles and questioning prejudices.

Rita has been returning to the stage in recent years, reminding audiences of her enduring talent and love of the performing arts. Her genuineness and audience-connecting skills guarantee that her theatrical achievements will be honored and appreciated for many years to come.

Rita Moreno left behind a legacy of brilliance, tenacity, and advocacy via her accomplishments in theater. She has shown the value of theater as a vehicle for social change and cultural expression via her work, which has inspired and enlightened audiences in addition to entertaining them. Her experience serves as a reminder of the value of representation and the cross-cultural nature of the arts, which can promote awareness and understanding of the wide range of human experiences.

Collaborations with Renowned Artists

Throughout her seven-decade career, Rita Moreno has received numerous honors, but her most brilliant partnerships have been with some of the most well-known performers in the entertainment business. These partnerships have influenced her career by broadening her artistic horizons and giving her the opportunity to shine beside the titans of the business. Rita enhanced her craft and legacy by contributing her distinct energy, talent, and enthusiasm to each project and by learning from the artists she collaborated with.

When she was cast in the 1961 movie *West Side Story*, it became one of her most famous partnerships early in her career. The Broadway musical was adapted into a movie directed by Robert Wise and Jerome Robbins, featuring some of the best actors of the day. Rita's performance as Anita is still regarded as one of her best roles. Rita was able to demonstrate her variety and emotional depth while collaborating with a strong group of actors, including Richard Beymer, George Chakiris, and Natalie Wood. Rita developed her acting and dancing abilities and learned to control her energy under the strict guidance of Robbins, who was well-known for his perfectionism. Rita's performance won her the Academy Award for Best Supporting Actress.

Rita collaborated on the 1952 classic "Singin' in the Rain" with Gene Kelly in addition to her "West Side Story" partners. Despite having a minor part in the movie, she had the chance to collaborate directly with one of the best directors and dancers in Hollywood, thanks to this experience. Rita was motivated and strengthened in her desire for performance perfection by witnessing Kelly's poise and accuracy both as a performer and director. Rita's movements were influenced by Kelly's reputation as a choreographer and performer, and working on a production as classic as this one provided her with valuable insight into the nuances of musical theater that she would use throughout her career.

Working with Marlon Brando, one of the most renowned actors of his period, was another crucial partnership for Rita. Rita took a supporting role in the 1954 film "Désirée," where the two first met on the set. Beyond only working together professionally, Rita and Brando had a turbulent and intense love affair that lasted for almost ten years. Rita experienced transformation through their artistic exchanges despite their tumultuous personal relationship. Having watched Brando, who was known for his revolutionary method of acting, she was able to refine her way of character development. His influence enabled Rita to break free from the clichéd parts that Hollywood frequently cast her in and embrace more naturalistic, emotionally charged performances.

Rita benefited much from Brando's influence as an artistic mentor as well as from his romantic partnership. She witnessed directly how Brando gave every character his all and was not scared to take chances with the script. Rita connected with this audacity because she was starting to challenge the limitations of being a typecast in her work. Their interaction reminded her of the value of acting honestly and the necessity of pushing the boundaries of the creative.

Rita kept working with a variety of talented people in the 1970s and 1980s, both on stage and in film. One of her best-known collaborations is with renowned writer Terrence McNally on "The Ritz." Rita won a Tony Award for Best Featured Actress in a Musical for her portrayal of the fiery Googie Gomez in this bizarre comedy. Rita was able to explore her comedic timing and theatricality thanks to McNally's witty and cutting writing, which gave her already extensive repertoire a new depth. Rita's skill as a multifaceted performer was highlighted by her ability to strike a balance between flashy comedy and a realistic, approachable character in "The Ritz," which was a critical and financial triumph.

Rita's partnership with the crew of "The Electric Company" on television gave her the chance to display yet another aspect of her expertise. This educational program, which ran in the 1970s, used humor, music, and sketch comedy to teach kids literacy skills. Rita had the chance to collaborate with other performers like Bill Cosby and Morgan Freeman because she was a frequent cast member. Even though "The Electric Company" catered to a younger audience, Rita was able to exercise her creativity once more. She was able to contribute to a production that had a significant social impact while combining her acting, singing, and comic skills.

Rita collaborated with directors and performers as well. She also collaborated with well-known composers and musicians, including Stephen Sondheim and Leonard Bernstein. Rita Bernstein's iconic Anita character would be accompanied by an outstanding score written by "West Side Story" composer Bernstein. Sondheim's lyrics for "West Side Story" provided Rita with the necessary material to depict Anita's humor, heartbreak, and resistance. She was a formidable presence in the musical thanks to her strong performances of "America" and "A Boy Like That," which highlighted not only her vocal ability but also her capacity to bring emotion to every word. Rita was encouraged to push her limits as a performer by working with such accomplished musical brains, which solidified her reputation in the musical theater industry.

Rita, later in her career, developed a long-lasting partnership with the renowned television writer and producer Norman Lear. Rita played Lydia Riera, a cherished Cuban grandmother with a vivid personality and a strong love for her family, in the 2017 revival of "One Day at a Time." Rita achieved yet another noteworthy milestone with the program, which humorously and heartfeltly addressed serious societal challenges. Rita was able to advance her support for representation on screen by collaborating with Lear, whose groundbreaking work in television is renowned for shattering stereotypes. Rita's warmth and comedic skill came through in the collaboration, which was a wonderful fit and contributed to the show's strong emotional resonance with both audiences and critics.

Rita collaborated closely with many talented artists in addition to Lear, like Gloria Estefan, who appeared as Lydia's sister in a guest appearance on "One Day at a Time." The show's inclusion of Estefan was a celebration of Latin culture, and the on-screen chemistry between the two performers demonstrated the potency of two powerful Latina women working together.

Rita Moreno's career is closely linked to her partnerships with well-known performers. She is an incredible performer now because of her capacity to change, grow, and learn from every partnership. Working with icons such as Marlon Brando, Gene Kelly, and Leonard Bernstein or conjuring up magic with modern visionaries like Gloria Estefan and Norman Lear, Rita's partnerships have enhanced her career and made a lasting impression on the entertainment business. Rita's persistent dedication to her profession and her unwavering ambition to push the frontiers of representation in the arts is shown by her willingness to take on new tasks and the mutual respect she has for these notable figures. Rita Moreno has strengthened her reputation as a famous performer and contributed to redefining what it means to be an artist in a world that is always changing thanks to these partnerships.

CHAPTER 6: AWARDS AND RECOGNITION

Oscar, Emmy, and Tony Wins

Rita Moreno's career is distinguished by a number of victories that cut across industries, decades, and cultures. Her Academy Award, Emmy, and Tony victories are among her most noteworthy triumphs; these honors set her apart as one of the select few performers to attain the elusive EGOT (Emmy, Grammy, Oscar, and Tony). These victories, however, tell a story of tenacity, extraordinary talent, and a never-ending quest for perfection. They are more than just significant achievements. Her place in entertainment history was cemented by each prize, which also represented her ability to shatter stereotypes in a field that frequently tried to limit her potential.

The Oscar Win: Breaking Ground in Hollywood

Rita Moreno created history in 1962 when, for her performance as Anita in "West Side Story," she was awarded the Academy Award for Best Supporting Actress. It was an unprecedented accomplishment for all Latina performers, not just Rita. Rita's triumph signaled a radical change in the perception of Latina actresses and the kinds of roles they might pursue during a period when Hollywood was known for locking actors of color into clichéd, one-dimensional roles.

One of the most bright and emotionally charged performances of the movie was hers as Anita. Anita was more than just a supporting character; she was a fierce, ardent, and genuinely human person. Anita reflected, in many respects, the difficulties faced by actual immigrants as they grappled with issues of discrimination, identification, and belonging. Rita gave the role a depth that captivated audiences with every move, every statement, and every emotion she expressed. Her performances in songs like "America" and "A Boy Like That" demonstrated her flexibility, fusing her acting, dancing, and singing skills into one unique, unforgettable performance.

Rita's Oscar triumph, however, was more than just a reflection of her skill; it was also a statement against Hollywood's pervasive typecasting. Rita had frequently been assigned clichéd parts before "West Side Story," such as the "exotic" or the "spitfire" Latina. Her Oscar victory opened doors for upcoming generations of performers and demonstrated to the industry that Latina actresses could succeed in challenging, multifaceted parts. Rita made history by becoming the first Latina to win an Academy Award, thanks to this momentous victory, which is still noteworthy today.

But it was a bittersweet victory. Rita thought that her path to the most coveted honor in Hollywood would lead to an abundance of challenging opportunities. Rather, she was presented with more of the same: shallow ethnic roles. This only made her more determined to strive for greater representation. However, even with her victory, it was evident that Hollywood still needed to do more to provide Latina actors with significant roles.

Emmy Wins: Shining in Television

Although Rita's Oscar cemented her legacy in cinema history, her two Primetime Emmy Awards showcase her exceptional adaptability and skill in television. She received her first Emmy in 1977 for her performance as a guest on "The Muppet Show." Even though "The Muppet Show" was geared for children, adults enjoyed watching it as well, and Rita's performance was a happy and lovely showcase of her musical ability and humorous timing. Rita sang the Spanish song "Fever" in her episode alongside Animal, the Muppets' untamed percussionist. Her performance was one of the most memorable in the show's history because of her interaction with the characters and her effortless ability to fit the whimsical, eccentric humor of the program. Not only did she receive an Emmy for her comedy skills, but it also demonstrated how well she could fit into any genre and media.

Rita received her second Emmy for a guest performance on the sitcom "The Rockford Files" just a year later, in 1978. One of the most watched television dramas at the time, starring James Garner, Rita garnered praise from critics for her portrayal of the eccentric, brassy call girl Rita Kapkovic. Rita stood out in a genre where female characters were frequently marginalized because of the combination of wit, vulnerability, and strength she brought to her character.

Rita's Emmy victories demonstrated her versatility as a performer, showcasing her ability to handle television with the same skill as she had commanded on stage and screen. Her popularity on the small screen helped her reach a wider audience, putting her in millions of American homes and solidifying her status as a cherished character in American popular culture.

The Tony Win: Dominating the Stage

Rita had already made a name for herself in theater and on screen, but it was her efforts in the latter that earned her the coveted Tony Award. Her portrayal of Googie Gomez in Terrence McNally's Broadway comedy "The Ritz" earned her the 1975 Tony Award for Best Featured Actress in a Musical. Her serious personas from previous TV and film roles were set aside for this job, which allowed her to embrace the broad comedy sensibilities needed for the part completely.

Rita used the role of Googie, an extravagant nightclub singer with grandiose illusions, from "The Ritz" to showcase her humorous abilities. Night after night, Rita's portrayal of Googie brought the house down with her charm, humor, and reckless abandon. Her vocal delivery, physical humor, and comic timing were all masterfully combined in her presentation. Her ability to convey heart and humor in a part that, in less capable hands, may have been pure caricature mesmerized the audiences. Rita, however, gave Googie more nuance and made her more than just a joke.

Rita experienced a personal victory when she won the Tony Award for "The Ritz." She had always had a deep passion for theater, so being acknowledged at this esteemed level in this genre was a confirmation of her extraordinary talent as an entertainer. The fact that she had won in a completely unrelated genre to her earlier work, demonstrating her versatility as a superb dramatic actress and dancer, as well as her amazing comedy ability, made the victory even more impressive.

The Significance of EGOT

Rita gained prestige after winning the Oscar, Emmy, and Tony Awards, but her 1972 Grammy Award for "The Electric Company Album" sealed her place as an EGOT winner. Her reputation as one of the most talented and adaptable performers in entertainment history was solidified when she accomplished this uncommon achievement. Rita's membership in this esteemed organization, which comprises fewer than 20 people to date, is a testament to the depth of her talents in a variety of media.

These victories—the Tony, Emmy, and Oscar—signify not just her achievement but also her pioneering work with actors of color. Rita Moreno fought for recognition of her skill and for being seen, heard, and acknowledged at a time when Hollywood and Broadway frequently ignored Latina women. Numerous actresses and performers, especially those from disadvantaged backgrounds, have found inspiration in her accomplishments to think that they, too, can overcome the obstacles in an industry currently plagued by issues of diversity and representation.

Rita's victories at the Oscar, Emmy, and Tony Awards are evidence of her unwavering commitment to artistic quality rather than the pinnacle of her career. Every prize symbolizes a distinct stage of her journey, an obstacle she surmounted, and a wall she conquered. Rita Moreno has consistently demonstrated that her skill is limitless, whether it is on stage, in a movie, or on television. Her reputation as an EGOT-winning performer will inspire future generations forever.

Legacy in the Entertainment Industry

Rita Moreno has left an enduring impact on Hollywood culture and beyond, her legacy in the entertainment business being both colossal and transformational, reverberating well beyond her accomplishments. Rita achieved more over her career than just a collection of honors, commendations, and cheers. It was a redefinition of what was possible for actresses, especially women of color, in a field that had historically ignored and marginalized artists who did not conform to a specific, Eurocentric ideal. Rita always saw success as more than just becoming noticed personally; it meant paving the way for others who would follow her, unlocking doors that had previously been inaccessible to Latina actors, and leaving a legacy of visibility, empowerment, and genuineness.

Rita's reluctance to accept these limitations at a period when many Latina women's roles were restricted to stereotypes and one-dimensional characters had lasting ramifications. Her performances constantly pushed boundaries and questioned the accepted conventions of representation, whether they were on stage, in cinema, or on television. She played parts that gave her the opportunity to depict women as complex, nuanced, and authentic—roles that were characterized more by their humanity than by their race. This change was noteworthy in a field where actors of color were frequently stereotyped into limited, frequently demeaning parts. Rita's body of work shows her insistence on the dignity and depth of the persons she portrayed—a determination to avoid being boxed in.

Rita Moreno's influence extends beyond the parts she played; she was a strong advocate for diversity and representation in both on and off-screen media. She was not going to stay a passive participant in an industry where her voice had always been marginalized. Rather, she pushed for parts that accurately represented the complex, real-life experiences of Latina women by using her position to fight for more inclusive storytelling. Beyond her professional life, she was an outspoken opponent of Hollywood's lack of diversity. She devoted her life to bringing attention to the structural obstacles that performers of color must overcome. Rita realized that her success entails a duty not only to her profession but also to the generations of artists who would carry on her legacy.

Her achievements in the entertainment industry go beyond just her performances; she also had a significant role in changing Hollywood's perceptions of women, Latina artists, and people of color in general. Rita Moreno came to represent tenacity and perseverance in a variety of ways. Even after the triumph of "West Side Story," she might have easily rested on her laurels, but she never gave up on her cause of change advocacy. Rather, she persisted in advocating for roles that were more varied and significant, as well as for the acknowledgment that Latina actors are capable of taking the lead and molding stories. She broke down barriers and turned into a role model for aspiring performers, proving that you could thrive on your terms without giving in to pressure from the industry to fit a certain mold or compromising who you are.

Rita's impact was also evident in the way she broadened the range of narratives Hollywood was prepared to produce. She contributed to making room for more varied tales by declining to play traditional or humiliating parts. Her popularity proved that readers were eager to read tales that captured the rich array of human experiences seen in the real world, and her emphasis on authenticity cleared the path for the more nuanced representations of Latina characters that we see today. Rita's revolutionary work is an inspiration to contemporary television series and movies that focus on Latinx lives. Every endeavor that aims to portray more inclusive, genuine tales carries her legacy, and her impact is still shaping how Hollywood views representation.

Her enduring legacy also greatly stems from her ability to transition between genres and media successfully. Rita Moreno demonstrated that brilliance could not be limited to a single kind of performance or venue. She demonstrated a flexibility that made her not only a beloved character in American pop culture but also a great artistic force. She succeeded in theater, television, film, and even music. By doing this, she pushed the boundaries of what was considered possible for a Latina actress in the business. She disproved stereotypes about the kinds of parts and environments in which women of color might thrive. Rita's career is proof of the value of flexibility, diligence, and a will to overcome obstacles. She demonstrated that having several talents was not only feasible but also essential for success in a field that frequently tries to categorize its stars.

Her position as a trailblazer is assured, as she is the first Latina woman to win an Academy Award and one of the few performers to earn EGOT status. Her achievements are historically significant, but what really makes her unique is how she assumed that role with poise and determination. She started acting as a mentor to new performers, always pushing them to be proud of their cultural identities and to pursue greatness in a field that frequently tries to minimize or disregard the contributions of underrepresented groups. Rita Moreno has contributed to the development of a climate in which aspiring Latina actresses feel encouraged to follow their passions without having to give up on their heritage through her advocacy and mentoring.

She is seen as a symbol of the continuous struggle for equity and representation as well as an icon of the entertainment business, and her influence transcends beyond her roles into the larger cultural consciousness. Rita's example continues to inspire as newer actresses and filmmakers pick up the baton of campaigning. Her legacy is a living one that is always changing as the business shifts and new voices take up her work. Her career's durability and lasting influence may be seen in the fact that she is still a prominent and active figure in Hollywood today.

Rita Moreno left her mark on the entertainment industry in all its forms. She serves as a reminder that ability can overcome obstacles related to age, gender, and race when it is combined with courage and conviction. In addition to providing audiences with decades of entertainment, she is a character who has fundamentally changed the industry. She leaves behind a Hollywood that is gradually opening up, reflecting the diversity of the world, and being more open to telling important stories.

CHAPTER 7: PERSONAL LIFE AND CHALLENGES

Balancing Fame and Family

For Rita Moreno, striking a balance between her work and her family was a delicate act that demanded perseverance, adaptability, and a steadfast devotion to both. It's a complex dance that many public figures find difficult to navigate. Rita's ascent to fame was accompanied by the hectic demands of Hollywood, including long days on the set, nonstop travel, media attention, and the unwavering pursuit of perfection in a notoriously cruel field. Amidst the flash and glamour of her professional life, which was full of honors, accolades, and groundbreaking performances, she was also juggling the equally difficult task of upholding her family's normalcy and relationships behind the scenes.

Rita's personal and professional lives have always been entwined because her career responsibilities and family expectations frequently collided. An unwavering concentration on success characterized her early career years. Particularly for women of color, Hollywood in the 1950s and 1960s was not known for providing balanced lifestyles. Rita's drive to shatter the stereotypes of Latina actresses meant that her job frequently came first and that balance was hard to achieve. She was negotiating a world that frequently left little room for the peaceful times spent with her family and required all of her imagination, energy, and enthusiasm. Rita understood, however, that her emotional stability and sense of anchoring depended on her family.

Rita entered a new level of stardom as her career developed and after taking home the coveted Academy Award for her performance in *West Side Story*. More chances as well as challenges followed. Not only can fame affect a person in public, but it also has a cascading influence on other facets of their life, including their family. Even the strongest relationships may be strained by the demands of living in the spotlight, and Rita had to deal with the idea that her popularity would affect the people she cared about. Setting a line between the Rita her family knew and loved and the Rita the rest of the world saw on film became crucial to her. Although she occasionally found it challenging to uphold, this boundary was essential to her sense of self.

Fernanda, Rita's daughter, played a major role in her personal life. Her already complicated life became much more convoluted after she became a mother. Motherhood could not stop her from working on movie sets, theaters, or television shows. Still, Rita prioritized making sure her daughter was loved, nurtured, and kept away from the more negative parts of celebrity. Rita had to figure out how to meet her professional obligations and be there for her child, just like many other working mothers do. It wasn't always simple. Rita tried to have a close, meaningful relationship with her daughter despite missing out on several important occasions and having to be away due to work commitments, understanding that their relationship would keep her centered.

Rita's marriage to renowned cardiologist Leonard Gordon, her late husband, was another crucial area of her life that needed harmony. In sharp contrast to the glamour of Hollywood, Leonard lived in a world of science and medicine rather than the entertainment business. Mutual respect and an awareness of the demands Rita's job had on their family life served as the foundation of their partnership. Rita found stability in Leonard, who was not only a supportive spouse but also gave her a feeling of normalcy that was frequently lacking in the hectic world of celebrity. They worked to keep their family at the center of their lives while navigating the highs and lows of celebrity life together.

But celebrity comes with constant pressures, and it's frequently difficult to distinguish between one's private and public lives. Rita had to deliberate about where her energy and time were directed in order to maintain this equilibrium. She made a concerted effort to make sure that her relationships did not suffer as a result of her celebrity. As she grew older and her priorities started to change, this became even more crucial. Rita's love of acting and performing persisted. Still, she also grew to cherish the more intimate times spent with her daughter and, eventually, her grandchildren, who brought her much pleasure and happiness.

Facing the demands of being a role model also required juggling celebrity and family. Rita was well aware for the majority of her career that she was a trailblazer, a Latina actress who had shattered stereotypes in a field that had long kept women like her on the periphery. Being a pioneer meant that she had obligations to her family, community, and fans in addition to her fans. Rita aimed to set a good example for her daughter, demonstrating to her that achieving success did not have to come at the expense of relationships or morals. She was aware of the demands made of her by the general public, who viewed her as a representation of tenacity and success at the same time. It was difficult for Rita to balance these two responsibilities, but she was always fully committed to her family and her work.

Some of Rita's busiest times in her career were also the times when the conflict between her family and celebrity reached its height. It wasn't easy to balance several tasks and her personal life at the same time, and there were times when she wondered if she could have it all. Rita, like many women in demanding professions, had to deal with the assumption from society that she should be able to handle everything with ease, but the truth was much more nuanced. Both parties made sacrifices: she gave up job prospects to be with her family, and work obligations prevented her from spending quality time with them. Rita, however, managed to handle these difficulties with poise and tenacity despite everything.

Rita realizes the significance of her family in influencing her legacy as she considers her life and work. Her relationships with her daughter, her grandchildren, and her late husband bring her the most satisfaction despite her amazing accomplishments in theater, cinema, and television. Family is a steady source of affection and support, but fame, with all its glitz and awards, comes and goes. Rita's resilience and dedication to the people she cares about are demonstrated by her capacity to preserve these relationships in the face of intense public scrutiny.

In the end, Rita's ability to strike a balance between her family and her notoriety is a testament to her morality, fortitude, and awareness of what really counts in life. She has demonstrated that it is feasible to go to the pinnacles of one's job while still fostering the bonds that keep one alive. In addition to her groundbreaking performances and cultural influence, she leaves behind a legacy of love, devotion, and the quiet strength that comes from understanding that your family will always be your cornerstone, no matter how bright the limelight becomes.

Overcoming Adversity

Rita Moreno's life is replete with instances of her theme of overcoming adversity, which helped to mold her into the courageous, strong woman the world recognizes today. Her story is a tribute to grit, tenacity, and the strength of self-belief in the face of enormous obstacles. Few are aware of the enormous challenges she had to face and overcome in order to achieve those heights, despite the fact that many are drawn to the glamorous highlights of her career—her famous parts, accolades, and groundbreaking accomplishments. Rita experienced problems from a young age, but she overcame them and used them as motivation to succeed instead of letting them defeat her.

Rita was born in Humacao, Puerto Rico, in 1931, and she had to overcome her first obstacles at a young age. Growing up in Puerto Rico during that time was not easy, particularly for a household with little money. Rosa María, Rita's mother, courageously chose to leave Puerto Rico in search of a better life for herself and her daughter in the United States. Moving to New York and uprooting yourself was a huge risk, and the adjustment was not smooth. Rita had to say goodbye to her extended family, her native country, and the diverse cultural background that had influenced her formative years. She stepped foot in a world where people spoke a foreign language, the streets were cruel, and society in general did not always accept people who looked or sounded different.

The difficulties Rita faced as an immigrant were great, as she was thrown into a strange world with strange traditions and, most of the time, bigotry. There were unique obstacles for Latina children growing up in 1930s and 1940s New York. A young Puerto Rican girl had few options and faced widespread discrimination. Rita tackled this head-on, fighting not only to become fluent in English but also to blend in with a community that seemed determined to keep her on the periphery. One of the first challenges she would face was this feeling of being an outsider, and it would return frequently during her career.

The school was its battlefield. Rita wrote in her memoirs how her Puerto Rican heritage, accent, and appearance were frequent sources of bullying and mockery from her peers. These early experiences could have easily broken her spirit of isolation, but instead, they strengthened her resolve. Rita learned the value of self-worth and the requirement of resilience from her early experiences with racism and prejudice. She started to realize that she had to stop depending on other people to approve of her if she was going to succeed. Regardless of what society thought about her role in the world, she would need to find her sense of self and confidence.

Rita discovered that her troubles were far from ended when she joined the entertainment business. Her ethnicity was seen as both a strength and a weakness during the casting calls and auditions that characterized the early years of her career. Rita was pigeonholed into roles that were dehumanizing and reductive in a Hollywood that celebrated stereotypes. She kept getting cast as the "exotic" character, whether it was the sexy seductress, the fiery Latina, or the anonymous island girl. Producers and directors seldom looked past her race, and the parts that came her way were a reflection of the narrow, frequently prejudiced perception of what it meant to be a woman of color in the profession.

One of the most annoying challenges Rita had to face was this typecasting. Hollywood took a while to realize that she had more to give as an actor than the little roles that were presented to her, despite her extraordinary talent, charisma, and adaptability. Being continuously cast in parts that did not fully represent her strengths was discouraging, to put it mildly. Rita, however, rebelled against these constraints rather than accepting this as her destiny. She resisted letting her race be the only factor exploited by the industry to define her. In the early phases of her career, she had to accept stereotyped roles in order to survive, but she did it with inner resistance since she knew that one day she would overcome these limitations.

Her casting in *West Side Story* marked a turning point in her career. Even though this part was still limited by the industry's perception of Latina women, Rita took advantage of the chance to give Anita more nuance and honesty. Her performance dismantled preconceptions and transformed a potentially one-dimensional part into a compelling, multidimensional character that enthralled viewers. Not only was winning the Academy Award for Best Supporting Actress a personal accomplishment, but it also represented a symbolic triumph over the years-long adversity that had beset her. Rita had demonstrated that she was more than simply a "type" and that she was a powerful influence in Hollywood.

Even with this degree of acknowledgment, hardship did not go away, though. She did not receive the barrage of offers that one might anticipate from an Academy Award-winning actress in the years that followed her achievement. Rita actually discovered that she was still limited by the stereotypes and shallow roles that were still accessible to her. It was a terrible realization that her potential remained unfulfilled in Hollywood, even beyond the limited parameters they had set for her. Rita, though, was done taking these leftovers from the industry. Rather, she assumed charge of her career and actively pursued roles in theater, television, and other performing mediums where she could fully express herself as an artist and spread her wings.

Rita's battle with mental health was one of her greatest personal hardships. Rita struggled with severe melancholy and feelings of inadequacy behind the spotlight and awards. Her self-esteem suffered as a result of the industry's persistent rejection and restrictions, and there were moments when she doubted her value as a person and an actress. Complicating these mental struggles were complex personal relationships, such as a turbulent on-again, off-again romance with Marlon Brando that left her emotionally spent. At her lowest moments, Rita considered suicide because the burden of her hardships had become nearly unbearable.

But Rita had the fortitude to overcome her hardships even in their darkest hours. She reconstructed herself from the inside out using counseling, introspection, and a fresh dedication to her work. One of the most potent parts of her journey is her capacity to face her demons and take back her life. It illustrates her tenacity as a person and as an artist who refused to let her struggles define her. She has frequently discussed her difficulties in public, utilizing her position to raise awareness of the value of mental health and to inspire others to get treatment when they are in need.

Rita Moreno's life serves as a textbook example of overcoming hardship. She has consistently fought back with grace, courage, and an unbreakable spirit, whether it was in the face of prejudices from a culture that tried to marginalize her, restrictions from an industry that didn't understand her worth or personal problems that threatened to consume her. Her narrative is not merely one of overcoming hardship; rather, it is one of metamorphosis, of seizing chances, and of utilizing suffering as a catalyst for achievement. As a result, Rita has inspired generations of artists and aspirants to pursue their dreams by becoming an icon for both her remarkable talent and her extraordinary drive to overcome.

CHAPTER 8: LATER CAREER AND CONTINUED INFLUENCE

Recent Projects and Activism

Rita Moreno has demonstrated her unwavering commitment to the arts in recent years, utilizing her platform to fight for causes she believes in and inspire change in addition to performing. As she gets closer to her nineties, Moreno is still a driving force in the entertainment business, always pushing the envelope and never slowing down. Her activism demonstrates her lifetime dedication to social justice, equality, and representation, while her recent efforts demonstrate her adaptability and desire to remain relevant in a world that is changing quickly.

Rita Moreno's role in the Steven Spielberg-directed 2021 version of "West Side Story" is one of her most important recent undertakings. Moreno's depiction of Anita in the 1961 original "West Side Story" shot her to international stardom and won her an Academy Award. She had the rare chance to revisit the narrative that had shaped a large portion of her early career thanks to this contemporary rendition of the beloved movie. However, Moreno was not playing Anita again; rather, she was given the freshly developed part of Valentina, a character that is a reworking of the original Doc. In addition to acting in the movie, Moreno served as executive producer, working with Spielberg to make sure the picture reflected the realism of Latino culture that the original version lacked.

Her part in the movie is a tribute to her history as well as evidence of her enduring power in Hollywood. In addition to bringing a new viewpoint to the narrative, Moreno's portrayal of Valentina portrays the depth of passion and knowledge that come with years of experience. Her appearance in the movie seems significant since it serves as a declaration of her voice's continued importance in the industry as well as a reminder of how far Hollywood has come since the first picture. As an executive producer, Moreno was able to influence the film's cultural sensitivity and make sure that Latinos were respectfully and nuancedly portrayed. After decades of arduous accomplishment, she now demands respect in the industry, and this degree of creative control is a critical point in her career.

Moreno has continued to work on television after leaving "West Side Story," most notably on the revival of "One Day at a Time." Moreno portrayed the colorful and intensely affectionate Lydia Riera in this 2017–2020 television series. Lydia Riera is a Cuban grandmother who lives in Los Angeles with her daughter and grandchildren. The program addressed significant societal topics, including mental health, immigration, and LGBTQ+ rights, giving Moreno the opportunity to combine poignant, serious moments with her humorous timing. Many people liked her portrayal of Lydia, which introduced Moreno to a new generation of younger admirers who might not have known about her previous work. With "One Day at a Time," she was able to portray a complex Latina character once more and trace the development of Latino parts on television, a development that Moreno had personally battled for her entire career.

Rita Moreno has continued to be a vocal supporter of diversity and representation in Hollywood, as well as her acting career. Her race has caused her to be stereotyped for decades and to have fewer possibilities. Therefore, she has utilized her platform to speak out against the systematic racism and sexism that still exist in the industry today. Moreno routinely speaks at gatherings and on panels about the need for more Latino representation in movies and television shows. She frequently uses her personal experiences as a warning about what happens when a community is ignored. She has also underlined the significance of intersectionality, pointing out that different people face various challenges as a result of the ways in which gender, race, and class overlap. In this regard, Moreno's activism goes beyond historical reflection to actively promote a brighter future for upcoming artistic generations.

Moreno has been active in politics and social justice in addition to Hollywood. She has made a strong case for immigration reform, women's rights, and mental health awareness. In 2020, Moreno utilized her position to speak out against injustice, inspire young people to vote, and become involved in activism during the global COVID-19 pandemic and the continuous struggle for racial justice following George Floyd's death. Her work is very personal to her because she has personally faced discrimination and knows how important it is to win equality. During this time, Moreno made a number of passionate public speeches in which she pushed people to understand the value of advocating for underrepresented groups and the strength of group action.

Rita Moreno has also participated in a number of charitable endeavors, leveraging her notoriety to draw attention to problems close to her heart. Her involvement with the Hispanic Scholarship Fund, which awards scholarships to Latino students nationwide, dates back many years. Being aware of how crucial education is in helping people escape poverty, Moreno has frequently expressed her conviction that knowledge can be a powerful instrument for empowering people. She has also given support to a number of groups that offer mental health services, especially to communities of color who frequently encounter additional obstacles in getting care. Her issues with mental health, which she has publicly acknowledged in recent years to de-stigmatize discussions about depression and therapy, make her activism in this area all the more important.

Rita Moreno's recent advocacy is notable for its unwavering refusal to allow age to be a barrier. In a culture that frequently marginalizes senior citizens, Moreno continues to be a bright and vocal figure. She has made public remarks regarding the significance of representation for older women as well as Latinos. Moreno has persisted in shattering stereotypes in a field that values young, demonstrating that one's age should never be a barrier to action or innovation. Even in her older years, she has embraced her role as a mentor and trailblazer for younger generations, and her enthusiasm and energy for the issues she believes in remain as strong as ever.

Recent endeavors and activities by Rita Moreno demonstrate the amazing development of her profession and her unwavering dedication to improving the world. She never stops inspiring people, whether it's on the big screen, in public, or via her advocacy work. She possesses a strong sense of perseverance and believes that art and activism can transform the world. She has stated multiple times in interviews that her work is not yet finished. Rita Moreno's purpose is still to fight for representation, speak up for the voiceless, and leave a lasting legacy of good change, even though her roles and platforms may vary. She is actively influencing the future in this phase of her life, making sure that the doors she kicked open stay open for everyone who follows in her footsteps rather than just thinking back on her past successes.

Mentoring the Next Generation

One of the most significant and long-lasting components of Rita Moreno's legacy is her role as a mentor to the upcoming generation of artists and performers. She is ideally situated to provide insight, direction, and inspiration to others who aspire to follow in her footsteps, having traversed a field rife with discrimination, stereotypes, and innumerable obstacles for those of color. Moreno has been more than just a trailblazer in her life; she has also served as a symbol of hope for aspiring performers, particularly those who identify as Latino or minority, and who look up to her as an example of what can be accomplished with hard work, ability, and determination. According to Moreno, mentorship is about helping young people develop the bravery and self-assurance to stand up for their identities, cultures, and goals in a field that is frequently cruel. It is not just about imparting technical information or giving professional advice.

Empathy is the foundation of Moreno's mentoring approach. She may be more aware of most of the difficulties faced by minorities in Hollywood, such as being pressured to hide their cultural identity, change their name, or take parts that reinforce negative stereotypes. Since she had to face these forces for a large portion of her early career, Moreno has made it her mission to make sure that aspiring artists are not alone in their struggles. Her main advice to the next generation is to totally and passionately embrace their background and never let a business that has historically silenced other views diminish them. According to Moreno, this entails pushing aspiring Latino actors to turn down parts that trivialize or minimize their culture, even when those parts appear to be the only ones available at the moment. She emphasizes that attaining popularity on one's terms, with integrity and self-respect intact, is a prerequisite for true success.

In his role as a mentor, Moreno frequently interacts directly with youth. She frequently takes part in speaking events, panel discussions, and workshops where she imparts her knowledge and wisdom to young actors. She is renowned for being open and honest about the difficulties she encountered and the sacrifices she had to make at these events. Still, she also makes sure to highlight the successes that result from perseverance. She reminds aspiring actors that their voices count and that by being true to who they are, they are changing the way the business perceives marginalized communities. Moreno wants them to feel that they are capable of being seen and heard, not just as performers but also as storytellers who have the power to change the narratives that have long ignored them.

Moreno also stresses the value of education in her mentoring, not only in the academic sense but also in the larger context of self-awareness and ongoing development. She encourages aspiring artists to study acting, hone their technique, and comprehend the history of the entertainment business, including both its successes and setbacks. According to Moreno, young artists can be better prepared to undermine the structures of exclusion that have endured for so long if they have a greater grasp of them. She also encourages people she mentors to keep improving themselves, emphasizing that success is a journey with many stops along the way. Every role, every audition, and even every rejection, in her opinion, is an opportunity to develop and hone one's craft.

The emphasis that Moreno places on mental and emotional health is among the most significant features of her mentoring. She is well aware of the negative effects that the entertainment business can have on a person's mental and self-worth, particularly for women and people of color who are more likely to experience discrimination and be under pressure to fit in or thrive in unwelcoming situations. Moreno is a strong advocate for getting help when you need it, whether it's from a therapist, close friends, or other emotional support systems. She has been transparent about her battles with mental health, including moments when the pressures of celebrity overwhelmed her or when she felt alone since she was one of the few Latina women in her business. Through her sharing of these stories, she provides young artists with a platform to admit their challenges and seek support without shame freely. In this way, Moreno guides the next generation through the highs and lows of their careers, teaching them not only the trade but also how to safeguard their wellbeing.

In addition to her one-on-one mentoring work, Moreno's support of youth empowerment has been strengthened by her participation in initiatives like the Hispanic Scholarship Fund. Moreno has contributed to giving educational resources and financial support to Latino students who want to pursue careers in the arts through this organization and others of a similar nature. She is aware that a lack of resources frequently holds back talented people rather than a lack of drive or aptitude, and she strives to break down such obstacles. Moreno sees these programs as investments in the entertainment industry's future. She thinks that by encouraging a new generation of artists to challenge the status quo and tell stories that capture the depth and complexity of their experiences, she can help cultivate diverse talent at the grassroots level.

Moreno has mentored performers and artists from various backgrounds, pushing for diversity in many fields. Her influence goes beyond Latino artists. According to her, ensuring that the stories portrayed on television accurately represent the range of human experience is just as important as expanding the representation of Latinos in the entertainment industry. She exhorts upcoming artists to consider the wider picture of the influence they wish to make, encouraging them to use their platforms to elevate others and give voice to marginalized groups. Moreno's approach to mentorship is always about cultivating a sense of responsibility among young artists—to themselves, to their communities, and the world at large—whether through her activism for women's rights, LGBTQ+ equality, or racial justice.

Moreno's mentorship legacy includes a strong emphasis on her belief that the next generation needs to be brave. She instills in young artists the values of questioning the existing quo, standing up to authority when required, and holding an industry that has been hesitant to change. She does, however, also encourage children to be patient because improvement might come in small steps. Throughout her career, Moreno frequently had to wait years between parts that really showcased her abilities, but she never gave up. She advises her mentees that persistence counts just as much as skill and that each little accomplishment should be rejoiced over since it takes them one step closer to their objectives.

The ultimate goal of Moreno's mentorship is to make the industry a better place than when she entered it. She has dedicated her professional life to dismantling obstacles, and she is now motivated to assist others in doing the same. Many young performers look up to her as a role model, and she has become not only an icon but also a source of guidance and inspiration due to her advice, encouragement, and readiness to share her hard-earned experience. The performances, narratives, and careers of the upcoming generation of artists—artists who are more varied, more powerful, and more driven than ever to carry on Rita Moreno's torch—will surely reflect Moreno's influence as the entertainment business develops.

CHAPTER 9: THE LEGACY OF RITA MORENO

Impact on Arts and Culture

Rita Moreno has had an incalculable influence on the arts and culture, reaching beyond the theater and film to reverberate beyond generations, professions, and cultural contexts. Her legacy has had a profound impact on American entertainment and global representation, changing the way people perceive people of color in the arts generally as well as Latina women in particular. With her groundbreaking roles in television and movies as well as her activism and advocacy, Moreno has changed the entertainment industry and raised the bar for artists from all backgrounds. The cultural landscape has been transformed, and millions of hearts and minds have been touched by her achievements, which go far beyond her particular laurels.

During an era when rigid stereotypes characterized Hollywood's handling of actors of color, Moreno's performances gave the parts she played depth and genuineness. She was frequently cast in "exotic" or neglected roles early in her career, which was a reflection of the industry's limited perception of Latina women. But she broke past these limitations with unwavering talent and perseverance. Simple themes that had been repeated for a long time by mainstream entertainment were challenged by Moreno's ability to give complexity and emotional depth to even the most one-dimensional parts. Her breakthrough performance in "West Side Story" as Anita marked a turning point in both her professional life and the representation of Latina characters in Hollywood. Anita was a completely formed character that inspired respect and affection. She was feisty, strong, and unabashedly Latina. With this performance, Moreno won her first Academy Award as a Latina actor and solidified her place in popular culture.

But her influence on the arts and culture extends far beyond the accolades and titles she collected. The changing currents of American cultural identity in the second half of the 20th century can be observed in Moreno's career. She became a symbol of tenacity and the struggle for representation in a country wrestling with questions of race, identity, and inclusion. It was thanks to Moreno's refusal to play parts that minimized her Latina background or reduced her to a stereotype that other Latina artists could come after her. Her accomplishment demonstrated that Latino brilliance could be boldly found at the heart of American culture, not only on its outside.

She proceeded to tear down barriers and broaden the cultural dialogue in the theater and television, which were further areas of her artistic influence. She rose to fame in the 1970s as a beloved regular on the educational children's show "The Electric Company," where she demonstrated her comic and versatile abilities. She was able to reach a younger audience with this portrayal, leaving millions of children with a positive impression of a strong, talented Latina woman. For a lot of people, Moreno represented the first Latina person outside of the preconceptions of the time. Her work on "The Electric Company" highlighted the value of diversity representation in children's programming by offering a vital counter-narrative to the sometimes limited portrayals of Latinos in the media.

Her contributions to theater further solidify Moreno's cultural relevance. Her Broadway career, especially in shows like "The Ritz," proved her dedication to expanding the parameters of representation both on stage and in movies. Being one of the only Latina actresses to be successful in both fields, Moreno opened doors in the live theater industry for artists from marginalized communities. Her Tony Award victory for "The Ritz" represented more than just a personal achievement; it demonstrated the importance and relevance of Latino voices and stories in American theater, making them equal to those of any other group.

In addition to her career as a performer, Moreno's support of underrepresented groups has shaped her influence on culture. She has a long history of speaking up in favor of civil rights, especially those related to the representation of Latinos in the media. Moreno used her platform to advocate for more diversity and fairness because she recognized that the entertainment business can influence public opinion. She campaigned for roles that accurately represented the range of Latino experiences and resisted the industry's propensity to marginalize or overlook Latino actors. A new generation of Latino writers, directors, and performers has been able to expand on the foundations that Moreno helped lay thanks to this effort.

The feminist movement and Moreno's influence on art and culture are closely related. She had to deal with the misogyny that was rampant in the Hollywood industry as a woman, and she frequently found herself in predicaments where demands of beauty and submission overwhelmed her talent. Nevertheless, Moreno maintained her autonomy and agency throughout, calling for recognition of her artistic ability. In the process, she turned into a role model for a great number of women in the entertainment industry who saw in her the potential to overcome the constraints imposed by gender stereotypes. She has become an advocate for women's rights and a voice for equality in all its forms because of her openness to talk candidly about her encounters with sexism, both inside and outside of the profession.

Over time, Moreno's cultural influence has kept changing. She has stepped into new positions in recent years that showcase her adaptability and ongoing significance. Her participation in the revival of "One Day at a Time" demonstrated her enduring popularity and capacity to lead cultural dialogues. She played Lydia, a Cuban-American grandmother in this series, with a natural ability to blend warmth, comedy, and ethnic pride. Moreno made a connection with a new audience by way of her representation; many of them recognized themselves and their own families reflected in her persona. This part once again demonstrated Moreno's exceptional capacity to elevate and humanize Latino communities' experiences, demonstrating that their tales are as universal as any other.

Furthermore, Moreno's influence on culture is increased by her involvement as advisor and producer on the upcoming Steven Spielberg-directed "West Side Story" remake. Her participation in this production is an extension of her longstanding dedication to dispelling myths and advocating for more realistic representations of Latino characters, rather than just a rehash of her previous successes. Thanks to Moreno's involvement in this project, the new adaptation will be relevant for a modern audience by taking into account the advancements and cultural sensitivities that have occurred since the original film's premiere.

Rita Moreno has irrevocably changed the arts and culture in every facet of her career. In addition to captivating audiences with her amazing talent, she has dedicated her life to fighting for the possibilities that she was frequently denied and giving future generations of artists the same opportunity. Her legacy is one of tenacity, activism, and a profound love of the arts, all of which have contributed to the development of a more diverse and inclusive entertainment sector. Moreno has demonstrated by her ground-breaking work that art can be a potent force for good, one that can raise societies, subvert social norms, and encourage millions of people to dream more than they have before. Rita Moreno's influence on art and culture is more than simply a historical footnote; it is a dynamic, living example of the transformational potential of narrative and the timeless value of representation.

Continuing Her Mission

Rita Moreno's path has been marked by constant development, adjustment, and a steadfast dedication to her work and her purpose. Her work is never done, despite the fact that she has received recognition and reaped the rewards of a prosperous career that most artists could only imagine. Rather, Moreno has seen each achievement as a step closer to her ultimate goal, which is to use her platform to effect long-lasting change and to tell more stories about marginalized populations. In her later years, Moreno is still as driven and committed as ever to carry on her legacy—not by resting on her achievements but by furthering her goals of representation, advocacy, and high creative standards.

Her commitment to dismantling barriers and altering the entertainment industry's perspective of underrepresented communities is at the core of her ongoing goal. Moreno has understood for a long time that the struggle for representation is not over. She is open about how far the business still needs to go, but she has also talked a lot about how far things have moved since the days when she was restricted to playing stereotyped characters. Although opportunities for Latina and other minority performers have increased, there are still few deep and wide roles that truly represent their lives. Now, Moreno's goal is not just to acknowledge and appreciate her own achievements, but also to make sure that the development she has already achieved does not stop or reverse. She keeps raising her voice and challenging the industry to write better, think bigger, and cast a more diverse cast.

Moreno's current participation in projects that question Hollywood's status quo and foreground Latino storylines is indicative of her dedication to this purpose. She is an actor and producer in the Steven Spielberg-directed 2021 version of "West Side Story", which is one of the most notable examples of this. This reimagining of the 1961 classic gave Moreno a rare chance to consider her personal history as well as the direction that Latino representation in cinema is taking. Although she portrayed Valentina, a character developed especially for the remake, her work behind the scenes was equally important to the production as her on-screen work. In his capacity as executive producer, Moreno collaborated closely with the creative team to guarantee that the revised film steered clear of the cultural blunders of the first and instead gave the Puerto Rican characters more nuance and realism.

Her participation in this endeavor brought to light an important facet of her mission: it is the duty of those who have succeeded to provide possibilities for others.

Moreno has frequently discussed the dearth of Latina voices in Hollywood's upper echelons of authority. Even though there has been progress—particularly with more diverse casts and stories being told—there are still not enough Latina directors, producers, or writers to influence the tales that are shown on film. Thus, Moreno's goal goes beyond acting; she is committed to fostering the development of a new generation of artists who will not only be the stars of their own films but also serve as writers, directors, and producers. She realizes that being in front of the camera alone won't bring about true change; she also needs to be seated at the table where decisions are made.

Her advocacy for social justice and equality, which she pursues through her work with many organizations and as a public speaker, is an essential component of Moreno's ongoing purpose. Moreno has never wavered from speaking up on the topics that are most important to her in her professional life. She has long been an advocate for change, even before it was hip. She has spoken out against racism and sexism in Hollywood and shared her experiences as a Latina actor. With the ongoing changes in the American political and cultural landscape, Moreno's activism has become even more urgent. She frequently connects her personal experience to more significant social issues when speaking out on topics like racial justice, gender equality, and immigration reform. Her campaigning touches on the rights and experiences of marginalized populations everywhere, not only in the entertainment sector.

An emphasis on mental health is another aspect of Moreno's ongoing goal; in recent years, she has emerged as a vocal advocate for this cause. She has been candid about her issues with mental health, including her initial experiences with depression during the height of her stardom. Moreno has worked to de-stigmatize mental health concerns by discussing her experiences, especially in the Latino community, where these subjects are frequently frowned upon. She has become a significant voice in the discussion of mental health because of her desire to be open and honest about her difficulties. Her current purpose is to empower the next generation to ask for support and treatment without feeling judged.

Moreover, Moreno's objective encompasses mentorship and education. She is aware that investing in the next generation of artists, activists, and leaders is necessary to bring about long-lasting change—rather than focusing only on individual success stories. In order to help young artists and performers—especially those from disadvantaged communities—advance their careers and inspire them to embrace their heritage and identities, Moreno regularly takes part in mentorship programs. She has a strong desire to make sure that upcoming artists recognize the value of remaining authentic in the face of industry pressure to fit predetermined molds. Her mentoring program focuses on building resilience and confidence in the face of an industry that is frequently harsh, in addition to teaching technical skills.

Her ongoing goal is also deeply personal; she is always changing and reinventing what it means to be a woman in Hollywood at a particular age. Through her acceptance of new parts and opportunities that showcase her unwavering passion for her craft, she overcomes the preconceptions associated with aging in the entertainment industry. In a field where older women are sometimes disregarded or marginalized, Moreno nevertheless commands respect and attention. She has demonstrated that skill and relevancy have no expiration dates, and her very presence subverts the stereotypes that frequently determine the paths taken by women in Hollywood. She serves as a constant source of inspiration for both aspiring performers and seasoned pros, showing them that passion and inventiveness never fade with age.

Moreno's ongoing goal is to leave a legacy. Although she is well aware of the influence she has had, she is not willing to let that legacy define her. Rather, her motivation stems from her wish to make it bigger, to make sure that the opportunities she has created would stay open for future generations. Her goal is to change the world, one tale, one performance, and one act of activism at a time. She is not simply interested in transforming Hollywood. Rita Moreno demonstrates that her work is far from done as she persistently breaks down barriers, coaches upcoming artists, and supports causes that are important to her. She is still a force for justice, a force for change, and a brilliant example of how to use one's position for the benefit of society at large. Rita Moreno will continue her mission with the same fervor, commitment, and fire that have characterized her career for over 70 years as long as there is work to be done.

CONCLUSION

When we consider Rita Moreno's incredible life, we realize that her story is more than just a record of her successes in the entertainment business; it's a meaningful tale that embodies bravery, resiliency, and the unwavering quest for justice and representation. Rita's life story, from impoverished Puerto Rican origins to becoming a multifaceted Hollywood celebrity, is an encouraging example of the strength of willpower and the influence one person can have on society.

Rita has handled the complicated complexities of identity, celebrity, and craft throughout her career. She uses her platform to modify narratives and promote the real depiction of various voices in media, constantly challenging the misconceptions that have dogged Latina actors. In addition to being a turning point in her career, her ground-breaking performance as Anita in *West Side Story* established a standard for upcoming artistic generations and brought attention to the importance of sophisticated, nuanced representations of Latino characters in theater and film. Rita's brilliance and her unrelenting dedication to raising disadvantaged voices are demonstrated by her ability to overcome the limits placed upon her.

Her story also highlights the value of campaigning and mentoring. Rita is a prominent character in the ongoing struggle for equality in the arts because of her commitment to developing young artists and her efforts to address social issues. She has encouraged people to speak out and get help by discussing her personal experiences with identity, mental health, and structural impediments. Her impact on people's lives and the discussions she has sparked about self-acceptance and representation are more significant indicators of her legacy than the accolades she has received.

As we draw to a close our examination of Rita Moreno's life, it is evident that her influence goes well beyond winning an Oscar, an Emmy, or a Tony. Her legacy is one of bravery in the face of hardship, a rallying cry for diversity and honesty in the entertainment business, and a reminder that narrative can sway opinions and promote understanding. In addition to enhancing our cultural fabric, Rita's contributions to the arts have set the stage for a more inclusive future.

Rita Moreno's journey's core challenges every one of us to consider our own stories and the roles we play in promoting justice and representation. Rita is a symbol of optimism and resiliency in a society still troubled by concerns of inequality, proving that art can effect change. Her body of work inspires us to question the status quo, give voice to those who aren't often heard, and have faith in the transformational potential of creativity.

We are reminded that Rita Moreno's tale is far from over as we honor her. She consistently pushes limits and defies expectations with every new endeavor, demonstrating that having a purpose and passion can have a significant influence. Her dedication to activism, mentoring, and artistic brilliance in an ever-changing world is a source of constant inspiration for anybody looking to leave their mark. Rita Moreno is more than simply a legend; she is a living example of the amazing things that can happen when hard work and skill are combined. Rita also leaves us with a poignant message: the struggle for equality and representation will never cease, and it is up to each of us to carry on her legacy.

www.ingramcontent.com/pod-product-compliance
Lightning Source LLC
Chambersburg PA
CBHW050305230526
45471CB00005B/2024